Teaching Young Scientists

Curriculum-Linked Integrated Units

Grades K–1

Written by Karen Clemens Warrick
Illustrated by Joyce John

Fearon Teacher Aids
A Division of Frank Schaffer Publications, Inc.

Editors: Vicky Shiotsu, Kristin Eclov, Christine Hood

Cover Illustration: Pat Wong

Book Design: Jonathan Wu

Graphic Artist: Randy Shinsato

© Fearon Teacher Aids

A Division of Frank Schaffer Publications, Inc.

23740 Hawthorne Boulevard

Torrance, CA 90505-5927

Fearon Teacher Aids products were formerly manufactured and distributed by American Teaching Aids, Inc., a subsidiary of Silver Burdett Ginn, and are now manufactured and distributed by Frank Schaffer Publications, Inc. FEARON, FEARON TEACHER AIDS, and the FEARON balloon logo are marks used under license from Simon & Schuster, Inc.

All rights reserved—Printed in the United States of America.

Copyright © 2000 Fearon Teacher Aids

Notice! Copies of student pages may be reproduced by the classroom teacher for classroom use only, not for commercial resale. No part of this publication may be reproduced for storage in a retrieval system, or transmitted in any form or by means—electronic, mechanical, recording, etc.—without the written permission of the publisher. Reproduction of these materials for an entire school or school system is strictly prohibited.

FE11025

Contents

Note to Teachers 4
Inside Each Unit 5

Unit One: The World Around Us
  Background Information and Literature Resources 6
  Activities 7–16

Unit Two: Awesome Bats
  Background Information and Literature Resources 17
  Activities 18–27

Unit Three: Peppy Penguins
  Background Information and Literature Resources 28
  Activities 29–39

Unit Four: Backyard Critters
  Background Information and Literature Resources 40
  Activities 41–51

Unit Five: Tide Pool World
  Background Information and Literature Resources 52
  Activities 53–62

Note to Teachers

Children are naturally curious about their world. They love to explore, solve, and ask questions. *Teaching Young Scientists* focuses on helping children learn through science and math—two subject areas that focus on experimentation and discovery. Five thematic units are presented in this book with easy-to-use suggestions for incorporating the topics into your daily curriculum. Activities throughout each unit are tied directly to student learning outcomes expected at the kindergarten and first-grade levels. However, there's no limit to the knowledge and skills that your students will acquire as they explore these exciting units!

The overall objective of each unit is to encourage kindergarten and first-grade students to begin "thinking like scientists," to ask questions, to work together to explore and study concepts, and to solve problems. Your role as the teacher is to foster children's curiosity and sense of excitement about the world. And you do that well already!

Inside Each Unit

Introductory Pages and Literature Resources
Each unit begins with a page of introduction and an annotated list of literature resources. Helpful background information for each topic is provided to guide you through your thematic unit. Important vocabulary words are italicized so that you can easily spot them and introduce them to the class if you wish.

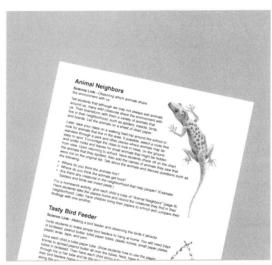

Activity Pages
The beginning activities of each unit present science and math concepts. Activities are designed with lots of opportunities for children to experience hands-on learning. They promote skills such as classifying, making observations, experimenting, and making models. Other activities in each unit integrate the thematic topic with language arts, social studies, music, art, and physical education.

Reproducible Pages
Each unit contains inviting reproducible pages that accompany some of the activities presented. Reproducible pages include diagrams, charts, patterns for art projects, puzzles, and more!

© Fearon Teacher Aids FE11025

Unit One
The World Around Us

Hop onboard and take your students on a tour of their neighborhood! Use activities from this unit to show children how people, animals, and plants share the same environment. Help students understand that many different kinds of people make up a community, and let them see that children as well as adults can be good community helpers.

Background for Teachers

The environment is the surrounding in which a person, animal, or plant lives. The environment includes both living and nonliving things. Wild creatures, such as birds, squirrels, and lizards along with a variety of trees, shrubs, and other plants, are part of a person's environment. Natural features, such as rivers, and man-made structures, such as buildings, also make up the environment.

A community is made up of a group of people who have something in common. It can be a place where people live or work. A community may be a city, suburb, or rural area. A city is home to large numbers of people, and it contains many houses, businesses, restaurants, and entertainment centers. A suburb is a residential area near a city. A rural area is made up of open spaces that often consist of farmland.

It takes many people doing different kinds of jobs to keep communities running smoothly. These people include community workers such as police officers, firefighters, doctors, and mail carriers. Communities also rely on individual residents doing their share in making the environment a safe and healthy place to live. As students explore their neighborhood, they will see that they are an important part of the community. They will discover that even though they are young and small, they can make significant contributions to their community.

Literature Resources

City Green by Dyanne Disalvo-Ryan (Morrow Junior Books, 1994). Marcy and Miss Rosa start a campaign to clean up a vacant lot and turn it into a community garden.

Night on Neighborhood Street by Eloise Greenfield (Dial, 1991). This book features poems about life in an African American community.

Round Buildings, Square Buildings and Buildings That Wriggle Like a Fish by Philip Isaacson (Knopf, 1988). Beautiful photos and poetic text capture the color, mood, and texture of the seemingly ordinary buildings in a neighborhood.

Where Does the Garbage Go? by Paul Showers (HarperCollins, 1994). The author discusses the growing problem of garbage disposal and how children can be part of the solution.

Animal Neighbors

Science Link—Observing which animals share the environment with us

Tell students that although we may not always see animals around us, many wild creatures share the environment with us. Then brainstorm with them a variety of animals that live in their neighborhood, such as spiders, insects, birds, and lizards. List the animals on a sheet of chart paper.

Later, take your class on a walking field trip around the school to look for animals that live in the area. If possible, select a route that wanders through a park and other places where animals may be easy to spot. Encourage the class to look in trees, on the ground, and under rocks and leaves for small animals that might be hidden from view. Upon returning to school, have students check off on the chart the animals that they spotted. Also add the names of animals they saw that were not on the original list. Talk about the animals and discuss questions such as the following:

- Where do you think the animals live?
- Where do you think the animals get food?
- Are there any creatures in the neighborhood that help people? (Example: Spiders and birds eat insect pests.)

For a homework activity, give each child a copy of "Animal Neighbors" (page 8). Have students take the papers home and record the creatures they find in their neighborhood. Later, have children bring their papers to school and compare their findings with one another.

Tasty Bird Feeder

Science Link—Making a bird feeder and observing the birds it attracts

Invite students to make simple bird feeders to hang at home. You will need trays of birdseed, peanut butter, toilet paper tubes, plastic knives, small paper plates, plastic wrap, tape, and yarn.

Give each child a toilet paper tube. Show students how to use the plastic knives to spread peanut butter all over the tubes. Next, have them roll the tubes in birdseed. Then have each child string a three-foot length of yarn through his or her tube and tie the ends together. Let students take their bird feeders home on paper plates. To protect the feeders along the way, cover the plates with plastic wrap, and secure the wrap with tape.

Have students hang their bird feeders outdoors in a place that allows them to remain hidden while watching the birds come to feed. During the week, have students keep track of the kinds of birds they see and how many. Later, invite them to share their results with the class.

Name_____ Date_____

 **Animal Neighbors**

Walk around your yard for 10 minutes. Look for animals that live near your home. (Do not count pets.) Draw them. Write their names if you know them.

_____   _____

How many different kinds of animals did you see? _____

Plant Collage

Science Link—Identifying the importance of plants in our environment

Take your students outdoors on a sunny day, and have them point out the different kinds of plants that grow around the school. Encourage students to notice the various grasses, shrubs, flowers, and trees. Take students back to the classroom, and list on the board the kinds of plants children saw. Then discuss the various reasons why people grow plants. (Examples: Flowers add color and beauty to a yard; fruits and vegetables provide food; shrubs and hedges serve as a boundary between two properties.)

Tell students that plants are an important part of the environment. Then talk about the following:

- Many plants provide food for animals as well as for people.
- Trees and other plants serve as homes to some animals.
- Wood, paper, and other products come from certain plants.
- Plants give off a gas called *oxygen;* people and animals need oxygen to live.

Later, have students cut out magazine pictures of plants. Have them find as many different kinds of plants as possible. Glue the pictures onto a large sheet of butcher paper to make a colorful collage.

Classroom Garden

Science Link—Examining how plants grow in their environment

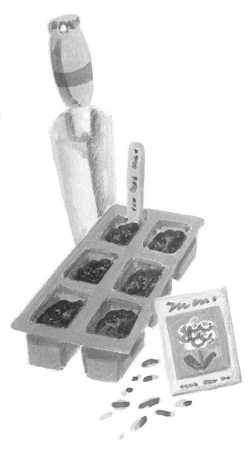

To prepare for this activity, consult a local nursery to learn which plants will grow well in your classroom. Then gather the things you will need to let students plant a small "garden" at school: a small plastic gardening tray for each child (available at nurseries), potting soil, foam trays (to place under the gardening trays), trowels, watering cans, and seeds.

Before letting children make their garden, discuss the things a plant needs to grow (soil, sunlight, water, air). Ask what would happen if any of these things were missing. (The plant would not grow; it would die.) Explain that a plant grows when the environment provides all the things needed for its survival. Then tell students that they can watch how plants grow by making a garden of their own.

First, fill the plastic trays with potting soil. Instruct each student to plant several seeds in his or her tray. Then have children gently cover the seeds with soil and and pat the soil down. Show the class how to gently water the seeds. Place the trays in a sunny location. Have students take care of their plants by watering them every day to keep the soil from drying out. Several weeks later, when the seeds have developed into plants, let children take their trays home.

© Fearon Teacher Aids FE11025

Trash Survey

Math and Ecology Link—Determining the amount of trash generated at school

Ask students how much trash they think their class produces in a week. Then tell them that they will be collecting "clean" classroom trash in garbage bags for a week. (Trash could include paper and fabric scraps, plastic wrap, and washed containers.)

Gather five garbage bags and write the following labels on them: *Paper, Plastic, Aluminum, Cardboard, Glass, Other.* Set the bags in one area of the room. During the week, have students separate their trash into the appropriate bags. At the end of the week, do one or more of the following activities:

- Have students carry the bags and determine which one is the heaviest. Let them weigh the bags on a scale, and then graph the collected data.
- Have students figure out how many bags of trash there would be if each classroom in the school collected the same amount as they did.
- Open one of the bags and let the class examine what was thrown away. Have students suggest which pieces of trash might be reused.
- Help students identify trash that can be recycled. Place those items in a recycling bin that can be picked up by the local trash company.
- Have students pick out any trash that can be reused for art projects. Place those items in a box that can be kept in your room for future use.

Recycle and Reuse

Ecology and Art Link—Identifying different types of trash, and reusing trash creatively

Discuss the meaning of "recycling" with students. Tell the class that certain kinds of trash can be collected and then cleaned and reused to make new products. Explain that recycling cuts down on the amount of materials we use to make products; this helps our planet, because we take less from the earth's natural resources. Recycling also cuts down on the amount of trash that needs to be burned or dumped; this cuts down on the pollution that results from disposing of trash.

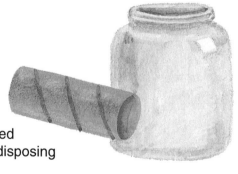

Next, give each child a copy of "Recycle and Reuse" (page 11) and talk about the different types of trash. If possible, bring a sample of each kind to show the class. Then have students take their papers home to do as homework. Later, have students bring their recycling projects to school to share with one another.

Name _____ Date _____

Recycle and Reuse

Here are some trash materials that can be recycled. Check off the ones that your family collects for recycling.

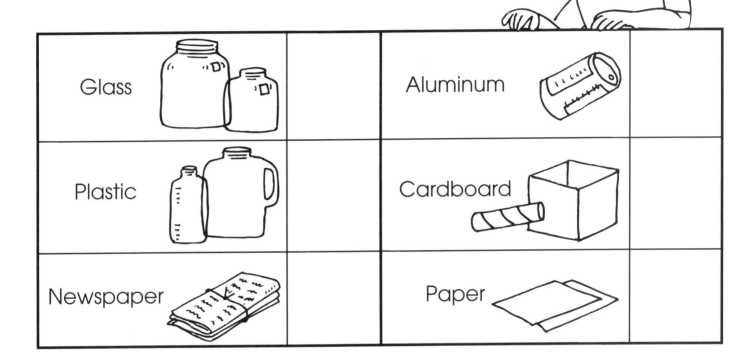

Pick out a trash item that can be recycled (Examples: glass jar or cardboard box). Make something out of it. Draw a picture of what you made. Then bring your item to school for sharing.

Recycled Garden

Art Link—Using imagination and creativity

Have students make colorful flowers from recycled materials. Ask them to contribute fabric scraps, buttons, foam packing materials, egg cartons, plastic lids, and other items for the project. Place the materials in a large box in one area of the room.

Give each child a tongue depressor to make the flower's stem. Have students use paint or felt markers to color the stem green. Then have each student glue a five-inch cardboard circle to the stem and write his or her name on the back of the circle. Then have students decorate the circles by gluing on recycled materials. Display their flowers on a bulletin board titled *Recycled Garden*.

Where Is My Neighborhood?

Social Studies Link—Reading a simple map

Get a simple map of your city or town, or draw one of your own on butcher paper. Display the map in front of the class. Tell students that the map shows a bird's-eye view of the community. Explain that if they were a bird flying above the area, the map shows what the animal would see.

Use the map to identify the street where your school is located. Write the school's name on a piece of self-sticking notepaper, and attach it to the map.

Next, take students outdoors on the school playground. Point out the directions *north, south, east,* and *west* to the class. Have students face north, and ask: *How many of you live north of the school? What else is north of the school?* Then have children face south, and ask: *How many of you live south of the school? What else is south of the school?* Repeat the procedure with the directions *east* and *west*. Take children back to the classroom, and point to the appropriate areas of the map as you ask these questions: *Who lives north of the school? Whose neighborhood lies south of the school? Who lives east of the school? How many of you live west of the school?* Then let children take turns pointing out on the map the approximate locations of their neighborhoods.

Community Helpers

Social Studies Link—Identifying ways that members of a community help one another

Brainstorm with students the different kinds of workers that make up a community. List suggestions on the board. If students tend to name only the more "well-known" workers, such as police officers, firefighters, and mail carriers, extend their thinking by asking questions such as: *Who serves you at a restaurant? Who works at a movie theater? Who helps you when your pet is ill? Who makes sure you're safe at a swimming pool?*

Afterwards, give students a copy of "Community Helpers" (page 14). Tell students to draw a community helper of their choice in the blank spot on the wheel and write the worker's name on the line. Then have students color the pictures, cut out the wheels, and attach the wheels together with a brad. Later, have students pair up and take turns spinning their wheels and stating one fact about the chosen community helper.

Community Workers Dress-up

Creative Dramatics Link—Role-playing as a worker in the community

Children will enjoy dressing up as workers. Collect a variety of clothes and props for this activity. You may be able to purchase some things inexpensively from stores that sell party supplies or costumes. Parents may also be able to contribute items. Here are examples of some things you might collect:

shirt and tie	large pouch filled with junk mail
briefcase	gardening tools
toy doctor's kit	gardening gloves
toy phone	cooking utensils
firefighter's hat	toy cash register
police badge	toy tools
apron	toy microphone
plastic foods	

Put the items in a place where students can dress up and role-play in their spare time. For more directed activities, try the following ideas:

- Have one student at a time dress up as a worker and tell you what his or her day is like.
- Ask one or more students to act out specific situations. For example, have one child pretend to be a customer at a restaurant and another pretend to be the waiter or waitress.
- Take a photo of each child dressed as a community worker. Have students dictate or write sentences telling the importance of that person's job. Display the sentences and photos together.

© Fearon Teacher Aids FE11025

13

Name _____   Date _____

Community Helpers

1. Draw a worker in the blank space. Write that person's name on the line.
2. Color the pictures.
3. Cut out the wheels. Place the wheel with your name on top of the other wheel. Attach the wheels with a brad.

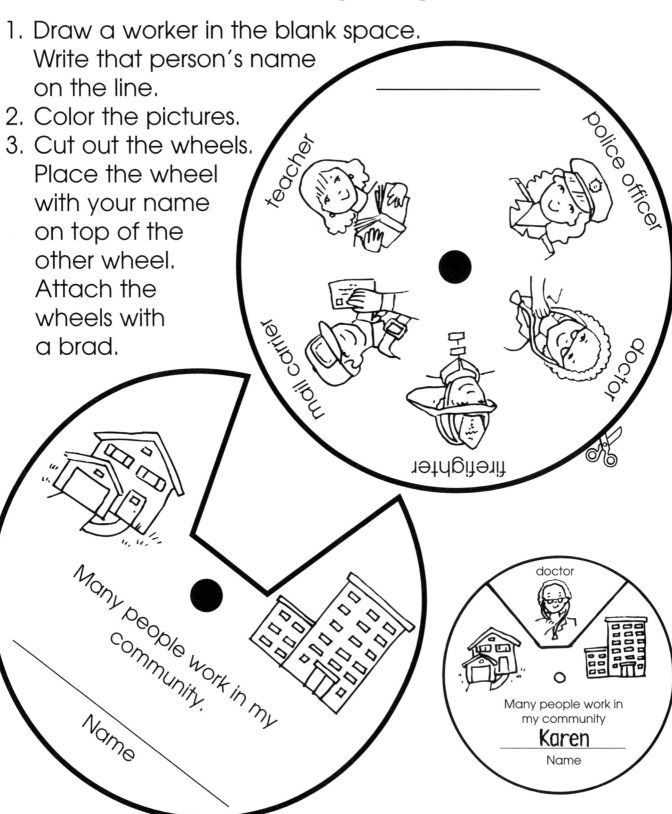

City Neighbors, Country Neighbors

Social Studies Link—Identifying different kinds of communities

Show students different kinds of neighborhoods (big city, small town, farm community). Discuss the fact that although these areas look different, they are all communities. Then talk about what communities have in common. (Examples: *They provide people with basic needs such as shelter and food. They are made up of people who live or work together. They provide people with ways to make a living.*) Next, discuss what makes communities different. (Examples: *Some communities have more people. Some communities have more buildings. Some communities have wide, open spaces.*)

Tell students that some communities are cities. Explain that a city is made up of many buildings and large numbers of people. Tell the class that the countryside, on the other hand, is made up of wide, open spaces and much fewer people. Then get two charts. Label one *City* and the other *Country.* Have each student find a picture of a community in a newspaper or magazine. Have students cut out the pictures and glue them onto the appropriate charts. Afterwards, have children explain how they decided on which chart to place their pictures.

I Can Be a Good Neighbor

Social Studies Link—Practicing good citizenship

Ask students what it means to be a "good neighbor." (Examples: *Be kind and polite to those around you. Help people and animals in need.*) Next, ask children what they can do to be good neighbors to the people in their neighborhoods. (Examples: *Help clean up a yard. Offer to help carry in groceries.*) Then ask what children can do to be a good neighbor in their school community. (Examples: *Be a friend to children who are new to the school. Help someone who gets hurt or bullied.*) Tell the class that people who live and work together need to get along and help one another if the community is going to be a safe and happy place.

Next, tell children that for one week they will perform one kind or helpful deed each day at home or at school. During that time, they will also see the responses they get from the people around them. Tell students that you will be doing the activity with them, too!

At the end of the week, discuss the results with the class. Ask questions such as: *How did people feel when you offered to help them? How did you feel when you were kind or helpful?* Discuss the fact that when people reach out to help others, the whole community benefits.

Changes in Our Community

Social Studies Link—Understanding that communities change

Tell your students to pretend that someone who lived in the area 100 years ago came back to visit. Ask what things that person might be surprised to see (Examples: *more buildings and people, less trees and less open spaces, new forms of transportation*). Ask students to name what kinds of changes are caused by nature (forces such as storms and earthquakes) and what kinds are brought about by people (factors such as new construction and new inventions). Tell students that the world around them is constantly changing, whether it is by the force of nature of the influence of people.

Next, discuss with children what their community might be like in the future. Ask how the community might change and in what way people's lives would be different. List students' ideas on the board. Then have them paint pictures showing what their community might look like 100 years from now. Have children write one or more sentences describing their pictures.

On the Go

Social Studies and Language Arts Link—Recognizing different modes of transportation

Ask students how they get to school (Examples: *walk, ride a bike, ride in a car or van, take the bus*). Then ask them if they have ever traveled elsewhere in a different way. Write those responses on the board as well (Examples: *plane, train, boat*). Ask students why people could not travel in planes hundreds of years ago. (Planes were not invented yet.) Explain that scientists and inventors have developed new ways of travel that people hundreds of years ago never could have imagined.

Next, get two sheets of chart paper. Title one chart *How People Travel Now* and title the other *How People Traveled Long Ago.* Have students help you fill in the charts with words and phrases, such as *walking* and *riding a horse*. (In some cases, a word or phrase will be added to both charts.) Then use pictures from encyclopedias or library books to show the class other forms of travel, and have students add more words and phrases to the chart, such as *stagecoach* and *helicopter*. After lists are completed, give students small pieces of drawing paper and assign each child a word or phrase to illustrate. Have students glue their pictures to the charts for a colorful display.

Unit Two

Awesome Bats

Introduce your students to the fascinating world of bats, and foster respect for one of nature's most misunderstood creatures.

Background for Teachers

Bats are found in all parts of the world except where it is extremely hot or cold. Most bats live in tropical areas where they can find food all year round. There are more than 900 kinds of bats. About 40 kinds of bats live in Canada and the United States.

Bats are mammals. Their bodies are covered with hair. Like people, they have live babies that feed on milk. Bats are the only mammals that fly. Their wings are covered by thin, flexible skin stretched between their fingers.

Many bats live in groups called *colonies.* These colonies may have thousands or millions of members. Some bats live in caves. Others live in trees, bushes, and buildings. A bat's home is called a *roost.*

Bats spend the day sleeping and go hunting at night. Many bats eat as much as half their weight in food in one night! Some bats feed on insects, scorpions, or spiders. Others eat fish, lizards, small birds, or tree frogs. The vampire bat feeds on the blood of other animals.

Literature Resources

Batwings and the Curtain of Night by Marguerite Davol (Orchard Books, 1997). This is an original creation myth that explains why bats hang upside down in large groups.

Cave Life by Christine Gunzi (Dorling Kindersley, 1993). This book discusses unusual plants and animals that live in caves.

Outside and Inside Bats by Sandra Markle (Atheneum, 1997). Children will delight in this close-up look at bats—from the outside in!

Shadows of the Night: The Hidden World of the Little Brown Bat by Barbara Bash (Sierra Club, 1993). Readers follow a little brown bat through a year of its amazing life.

Stellaluna by Janell Cannon (Harcourt Brace, 1993). A baby fruit bat is separated from its mother.

Zipping, Zapping, Zooming Bats by Ann Earle (HarperCollins, 1995). The author reveals the world of bats—dispelling common myths and revealing the vital role of bats in our environment.

What Are Bats Really Like?

Science Link—Learning information about bats

Get a library book that features bats. Gather students around you on the floor. Darken the room to set the mood. Show a picture of a bat, and ask questions such as: *How does seeing a bat make you feel? Are you afraid of bats? Why or why not? Have you ever seen a bat?* Tell the class that many people are afraid of bats. Explain that people often have misconceptions about bats:

- *Bats are blind.* Tell the class that all bats can see.
- *Bats will try to fly into your hair.* Explain that bats are shy creatures that avoid people.
- *Bats are dirty.* Bats are clean animals. Like cats, they spend a lot of time grooming themselves.
- *Bats carry rabies.* Few bats carry rabies. Tell children, however, that it is not a good idea to touch a bat lying on the ground. Explain that the bat might be sick and may bite if frightened.

Tell students that one of the reasons people have false ideas about bats is that they really do not know what these animals are like. Then choose a simple picture book about bats to read to your class. (Janell Cannon's *Stellaluna* is a good choice for young children.) Keep the room dim and read by flashlight. Ask students to listen while you read to see if they can learn what bats are really like. After reading the book, have students state what facts they learned. Write their responses on the board. Then have each child illustrate a fact and write a corresponding sentence. Display drawings on a bulletin board.

A Bat Is Like Me

Science Link—Comparing and contrasting bats and people

Show pictures of bats to students, and have them describe the animals. Tell them that though bats look different from people, the two are alike in many ways. Explain that bats are mammals, just like people. Then give students the following information about mammals: *Mammals have hair or fur. They give birth to live young and feed them milk. Mammals protect and train their young more than do other animals. They are warm-blooded; that means their body temperature stays the same even though the temperature around them changes.*

Next, get a sheet of butcher paper, and draw a bat on the left side and a child on the right. Draw two interlocking circles below the pictures to make a Venn diagram. Then have children suggest words that describe bats, words that describe people, and words that describe both. Write their ideas on the Venn diagram, as shown.

A Bat's Body

Science Link—Identifying different parts of a bat

Tell the class that bats have bodies similar to the those of people and other mammals. Show pictures of bats, and point out the following:

- A bat has two ears, a nose, and a mouth.
- A bat has hands with fingers and feet with toes.
- A bat's wings are really its hands! The wings are made up of two thin layers of skin stretched between the bat's long fingers.
- A bat has sharp teeth.
- Many bats have a tail.
- A bat has weak legs. Some bats use their arms and legs to walk. Other bats do not walk at all. They use their legs to hang upside down from their roost (home).

For a follow-up activity, give each child a copy of "A Bat's Body" (page 20). Have students cut out the labels and glue them to the appropriate parts of the picture.

Different Kinds of Bats

Science Link—Learning about the features of different bats

Show the class pictures of different kinds of bats, and discuss their features. Have students notice that some bats have short ears while others have long ears. Some have longer tails than others. Some bats have unusual faces; the tube-nosed fruit bat, for example, has nostrils that look like straws.

Afterwards, give each child a copy of "My Mini-Book About Bats" (page 21). Have each student make a mini-book about bats. Instruct the children to color the pages and cut them out. Staple the pages together in order. Let students take their books home to share with their families.

© Fearon Teacher Aids FE11025

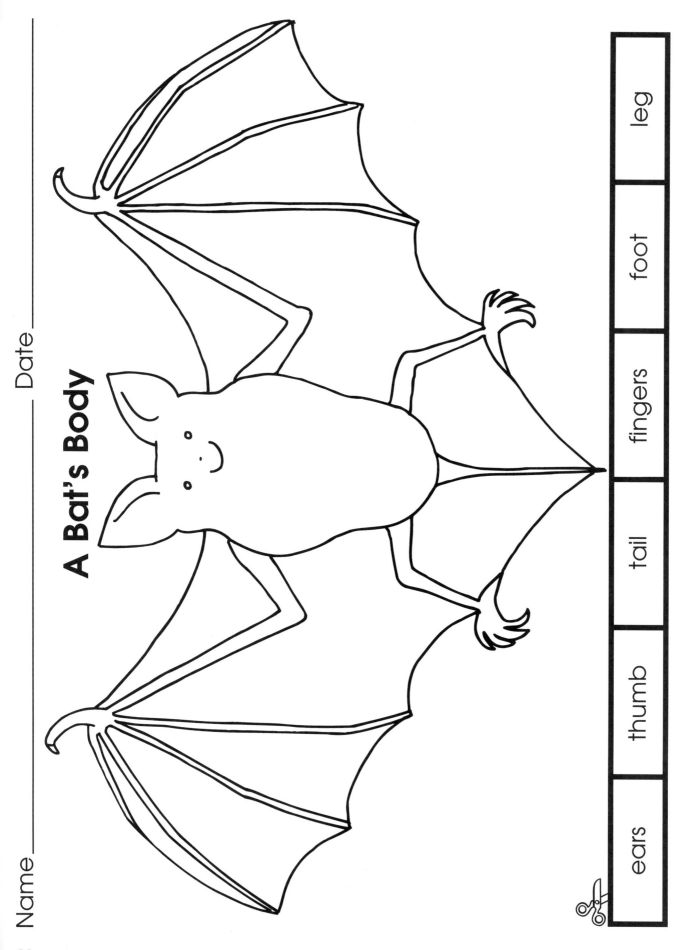

My Mini-Book About
Bats

Name _____

1

Some bats have long ears.

2

Some bats have long tails.

3

Some bats have long tongues.

4

Some bats have wrinkly faces.

5

Some bats have funny noses.

How Wide Can You Stretch?

Math Link—Measuring length

Tell the class that bats come in different sizes. The smallest bat, the Kitti's hog-nosed bat of Thailand, is about the size of a bumblebee. Explain that a bumblebee is about one-half inch to one inch long. Tell students that the largest bat, called the *flying fox,* has a wingspan of six feet. Explain that a wingspan measures the width of a bat with outstretched wings, from one end to the other end. Add that many North American bats have a wingspan of about one foot.

Next, do this measuring activity to show children the difference between one inch, one foot, and six feet. Lay out a length of yarn on a table or on the floor. Call on a child to measure and cut one inch of the yarn. Then ask another child to measure and cut a one-foot length of yarn. Finally, have a third child measure and cut a six-foot length. Tape the pieces to a sheet of butcher paper so that students can compare them. Discuss the fact that the yarn represents different sizes of bats.

For a follow-up activity, have children measure themselves to see how wide they can stretch out with their arms. Divide the class into pairs, and give each pair a tape measure. Have partners measure each other's outstretched arms, measuring from the middle finger of one hand to the middle finger of the other. Record the measurements on a chart with each child's name. Afterwards, discuss the following:

- Who had the widest span?
- Who had the least span?
- Whose measurement was closest to the wingspan of a flying fox?
- Do you think taller people can stretch their arms farther than shorter people? How could we test this?

Batty Math

Math Link—Adding and subtracting with bat manipulatives

Your students will have fun practicing addition and subtraction with this activity! First, reproduce "Batty Math" (page 24) for each child, and instruct children to color and cut out the bats. Then do the following activities:

- Give story problems for the class to solve using their bat and cave pictures. Here are some examples of problems you can try:
  There were 3 bats in the cave. Then 2 more bats came. How many bats were there altogether?
  There were 6 bats sleeping in the cave. Then 1 bat flew away. How many bats were left in the cave?
  There were 7 bats in the cave and 3 bats outside. How many more bats were in the cave than there were outside?
- Have each student work with a partner. Let children take turns dictating a story problem for their partners to solve.

Batty Poetry

Language Arts Link—Using colorful language

Try this creative writing activity when your students have become familiar with bats. First, discuss bats and the way they look. Have the class suggest words and phrases that describe their appearance, and write their ideas on the board. Next, have them suggest *-ing* words that describe a bat's actions, such as *flying, swooping,* or *hanging.* Then have children give phrases commenting about bats; for example, they could state what they think about bats. Finally, have the class suggest words (nouns) that could be used in place of the word *bat,* such as *furry creature.* When all suggestions have been made, have students work with all the ideas they generated to compose a class poem about bats. Use the following structure:

Name of animal	Bats
Two words describing bats	Mysterious, quiet,
Three *-ing* words describing what bats do	Gliding, swooping, hanging,
A phrase that gives an opinion about bats	They fill me with awe,
A synonym for *bat*	Furry flyers.

Write the poem on a sheet of chart paper. Have children cut out small bats from black paper, and decorate the chart with their paper cutouts.

© Fearon Teacher Aids FE11025

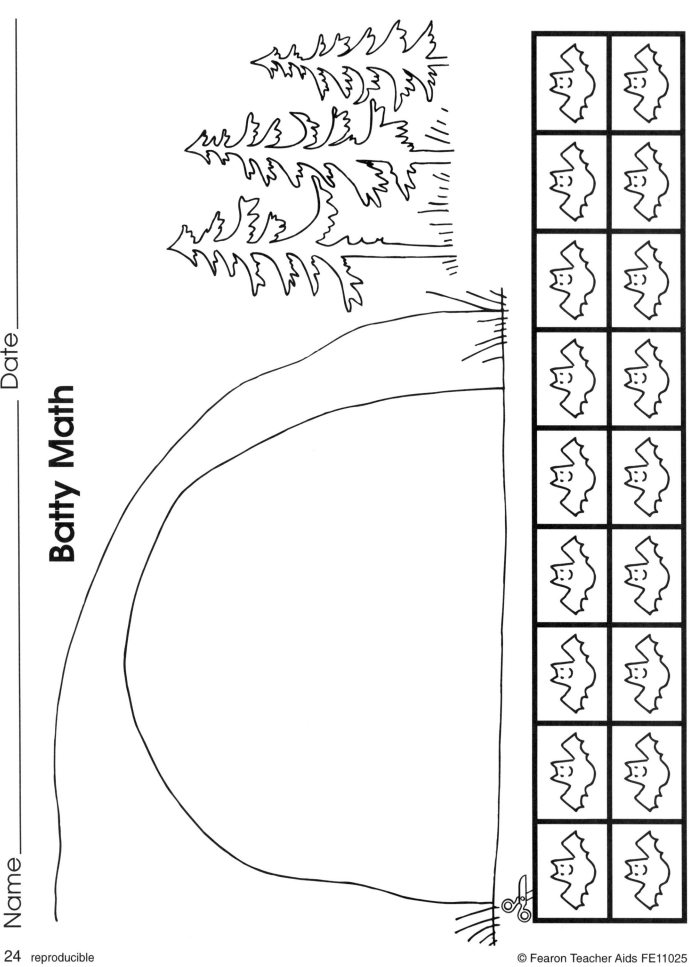

Bat Phonics

Language Arts Link—Distinguishing -at words

Cut out the bat pattern on page 26. Use it to cut eight bats from black paper. Write the word *bat* with a white-colored pencil on one shape. Tape the bat to the board.

Read the word *bat* with students, and have them notice the short *a* sound. Then have them suggest other words that rhyme with *bat,* and write them with the white pencil on the other bat shapes *(cat, fat, hat, mat, pat, rat, sat).* Tape the words to the board.

Give the class riddles about -at words, such as: *This is an animal with two pointed ears and four paws.* Have students guess the answer and point out the corresponding bat. Continue until you have given riddles about all the words on the board. For an extra challenge, let children make up their own riddles to ask the class.

A Bat Puppet

Art Link—Creating a decorative puppet

Use the pattern on page 26 to make black paper bats. Give a bat to each student. Then have students decorate their bats with materials such as colored pencils, bits of colored paper, sequins, and glitter. Have students glue a craft stick to the back of their bats to make puppets. Afterwards, let each child hold up his or her bat to the class and state one fact about bats.

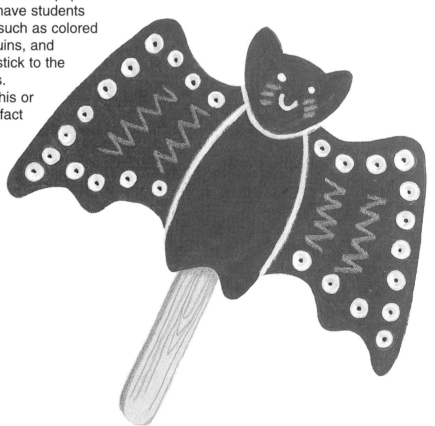

© Fearon Teacher Aids FE11025

Name _____

Date _____

Bat Pattern

26 reproducible © Fearon Teacher Aids FE11025

Bat Dioramas

Art Link—Making a three-dimensional display

Let students make a colorful shoe-box diorama, showing a bat's natural habitat. First, have children use paint or colored paper to decorate the inside of the box to resemble a cave, forest, or other environment. Show students how to make rocks, trees, and other features stand up by first drawing them on paper, cutting them out, and folding the bottom portion, as shown. Have children glue these features to the inside of the box.

Next, have students draw and cut out several bats. Have them suspend the bats from the top of their diorama using thread and tape.

Flapping Bat Wings

Creative Movement Link—Using colorful language

For this movement activity, you will need to push tables and chairs away from the center of the classroom. You will also need background music.

Spread children out around the room and have them sit on the floor. Ask students to close their eyes and imagine that they have wings like a bat. Have them fold their arms along the sides of their bodies like sleeping bats. Then turn the lights down low. Tell the class that you will be playing music softly for them as they "sleep" in their "caves."

Play the music softly for a minute, and then let it get louder. Have children "fly" around the room for a couple of minutes. (Remind the class that bats fly silently and without bumping into things.) Then gradually lower the volume of the music, and let children return to their caves. When all students are in their sitting positions, turn off the music as a signal for them to fold their wings and "go to sleep."

© Fearon Teacher Aids FE11025

Unit Three

Peppy Penguins

Use the ideas in this unit to help you take your class on an exciting expedition to the South Pole! Your students will marvel at penguins and their lively antics!

Background for Teachers

Penguins live only in the southern hemisphere. Several live in the icy regions of Antarctica. The smallest penguin is about one foot high, while the largest—the emperor penguin—stands four feet high. Penguins have stocky bodies and short, thick feathers. Their feathers are white on the belly and black on the back. Some have brightly-colored patches on their necks.

Penguins waddle awkwardly on land except when they lie flat on their bellies and slide down snowy slopes like a toboggan. Penguins cannot fly. Their wings, unlike the wings of other birds, have developed into flippers that serve as paddles in the water. Their flippers and their webbed feet help penguins swim and dive. Their waterproof coat and thick layers of fat protect them in frigid water.

Penguins spend most of their lives in water, but they come on land to lay eggs and raise their young. They make nests in large colonies called *rookeries.* A rookery may have as many as one million birds! Both the mother and father penguin are devoted to their young. One parent always stands guard, while the other brings fish for the babies. The baby takes the food by pushing its beak down the parent's throat. Young penguins are able to look after themselves at about six months of age.

Literature Resources

Antarctica by Helen Cowcher (Farrar, Straus and Giroux, 1990). Bold, dramatic pictures and moving text describe Antarctica's environment from the penguins' vantage point.

The Penguin by Anne-Marie Dalmais (Rourke, 1983). This colorful book gives children an intriguing glimpse into the world of penguins.

Penguin Pete, Ahoy! by Marcus Pfister (North-South Books, 1993). Children will enjoy reading about Penguin Pete's adventure with his new friend, Horatio the mouse. Other books in this series include *Penguin Pete* and *Penguin Pete and Pat.*

Polar Wildlife by Kamini Khanduri (Scholastic, 1995). An introduction to polar plants and animals, with realistic illustrations.

This Place Is Cold by Vicki Cobb (Walker & Company, 1989). Pictures and text give students a tour of a very cold place.

Waterproof Coat

Science Link—Experimenting to find out how coated feathers protect penguins

Use this simple experiment to help students understand how a penguin's feathers help protect it in water. Students will need a 4" square of waxed paper, a 4" square of paper towel, and a small container of water.

Give students the following directions:

1. Dip your finger in the water. Then drop some water on each square.

2. Watch what happens to each piece of paper.

Students will observe that the water is absorbed by the paper towel but not by the waxed paper. Tell the class that the water soaked into the paper towel quickly. Explain that in the same way, cats and other animals that do not have waterproof coats get wet and cold quickly because the water soaks into their bodies. Tell the class that penguins, on the other hand, have a coating over their feathers, much like the waxed paper. Explain that the wax coating on the paper prevents the water from soaking in; in the same way, a penguin's feathers are coated with oil, giving the animal a waterproof coat that protects it in water.

Small, Stiff Wings

Science Link—Experimenting to find out how coated feathers protect penguins

Have the class try this experiment to see how a penguin's wings help it swim:

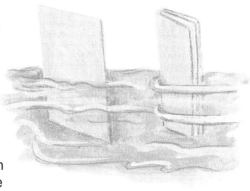

Give each child two sheets of drawing paper. Instruct children to fold one sheet of paper in half three times to form a long, thin rectangle. Next, fill a tub or sink with water. Have children try to paddle the water with their unfolded sheet of paper. Then have them try paddling with the folded paper. Students will see that the folded paper pushes the water better.

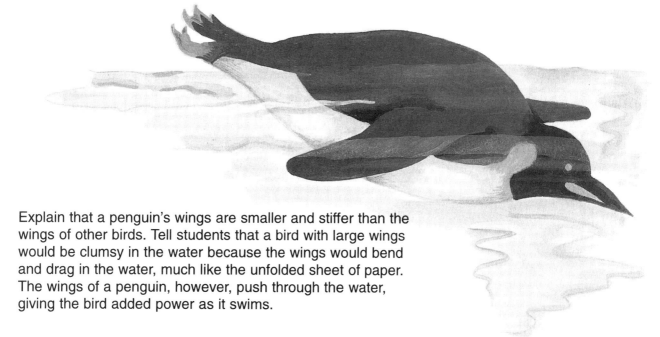

Explain that a penguin's wings are smaller and stiffer than the wings of other birds. Tell students that a bird with large wings would be clumsy in the water because the wings would bend and drag in the water, much like the unfolded sheet of paper. The wings of a penguin, however, push through the water, giving the bird added power as it swims.

Icy Habitat

Science Link—Creating a model to illustrate a natural environment

Tell the class that several kinds of penguins live in Antarctica, a large land area (continent) that surrounds the South Pole. Then use library books, encyclopedias, or other resources to show pictures of Antarctica to students. Ask them to describe the area, and write their ideas on the board. Share the following information with the class:

- Antarctica is almost completely covered by ice and snow.
- There are strong, cold winds.
- There are high mountain peaks and bare rocky areas.
- Temperatures are almost always below freezing (below 32° F).
- The waters around Antarctica are filled with icebergs and sheets of ice.

Remind students that penguins are well suited to their cold environment. (See the activities described on page 29.) Then tell students that they will create a mural that will transform part of their classroom into an icy "penguins' world." Roll a large piece of butcher paper on the floor, and have children kneel along one edge. Or, divide the class into five groups, and give each group a large sheet of paper. Provide library books and other reference materials with pictures of Antarctica. Have children draw pictures of ice, snow, water, and cliffs to create snowy backgrounds for their murals. Have them add pictures of penguins in the foreground. Encourage students to show the penguins doing a variety of activities, such as swimming, diving, sliding on ice, walking, and leaping. Let children look through reference materials for ideas on the kinds of things penguins do. When the pictures are finished, display them along one wall of the classroom.

Dressed for the Cold

Science and Social Studies Link—Classifying different types of clothing

Bring to class a variety of summer clothes (such as shorts, a T-shirt, and a swimsuit) and a variety of winter clothes (such as a scarf, pair of mittens, and thick jacket). Leave the clothes at a center where students can sort them into summer and winter clothes. After all children have had a chance to work at the center, ask them to explain how they knew which article of clothing was meant for which kind of weather. (Example: Winter clothes are made of thick materials.) Tell students that a penguin's body helps it stay comfortable in freezing temperatures, but that a person relies on clothing to survive the cold.

Next, give each child a copy of "Dressed for the Cold" (page 31). Tell students to imagine that they are going on a trip to visit some penguins at the South Pole. Have students read the page and color the appropriate pictures. Then have each child draw a picture of him- or herself dressed for a trip to Antarctica.

© Fearon Teacher Aids FE11025

Name _____ Date _____

Dressed for the Cold

Penguins don't have to dress for the cold, but you do! Color the pictures of the clothes that will keep you warm in the snow.

On the back of this paper, draw yourself dressed for a trip to Antarctica.

© Fearon Teacher Aids FE11025

Penguin Eggs

Math Link—Counting by twos

Tell the class that penguins spend most of their time in the water, but that they come on land to lay eggs and raise their young. Add that most penguin mothers lay two eggs at a time, although some may lay three. (The emperor penguin lays one egg at a time.) Then have students practice counting by twos with plastic eggs. Call on one student to stand in front of the room and hold two eggs. Write the number *2* on the board. Then call on another student with two more eggs to stand beside the first child. Have the class count *four,* and write the number *4* on the board. Continue the activity until you have at least ten children at the front of the room. (For an extra challenge, repeat the activity, but have children stand with three plastic eggs and let the class practice counting by threes.) For a follow-up, assign children to complete the activity sheet "Penguin Eggs" (page 33).

Penguin Parents

Social Studies Link—Comparing penguin parents and human parents

Tell the class that both the mother and father penguin help raise the young. Then give the following information:

- The emperor penguin mother lays a single egg on bare ice. She returns to the water, and the egg is watched by the father until it hatches. To keep the egg warm, the father rolls it onto his feet and covers it with a flap of skin on the lower part of his belly.
- Father emperor penguins huddle together to keep their eggs warm. They stay like this for two months. During this time, they do not eat. When the eggs hatch, the mothers return to care for the babies. The fathers go out to sea in search of food for themselves and their babies. The chicks stay warm under their mothers' bellies.
- Emperor penguins herd their chicks into a group. The adults then surround them to keep them warm.
- Penguin parents spend most of their time finding food for their chicks and feeding them.
- After six months, young penguins are able to care for themselves.

After sharing the above information with the class, discuss the following questions with students: *How are penguin parents and human parents alike? What responsibilities do each share? What responsibilities do penguin fathers and human fathers share? How are penguin babies and human babies alike?* Have the class help you make a chart comparing penguin parents and human parents, and penguin babies and human babies.

Name _____

Date _____

Penguin Eggs

How many eggs are there in all? _____

How many mother penguins are there in all? _____

Penguin Maze

Movement Link—Using motor skills to follow a maze

Review with the class that penguin parents both care for their young. (See the "Penguin Parents" activity on page 32.) Remind students that the father and mother take turns caring for the baby on land while the other looks for food in the water; the parent in the water returns with food for the chick.

Next, let students work together to create their own "penguin maze" on the floor with wooden blocks or masking tape. Cut out an oval "ocean" from blue paper, and lay it at one end of the maze. Cut out a "land" shape from brown paper, and lay it at the other end. Let students take turns going from the ocean through the maze to the land.

For follow-up, give each child a copy "Penguin Maze" (page 35) to complete.

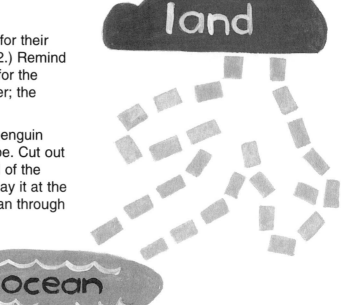

Penguin Mobile

Science and Art Link—Making a display of different kinds of penguins

Show library books and other resources that feature different kinds of penguins. Discuss the various features. Then pass out a copy of "Penguin Mobile" (page 36) to each child, and have children make a mobile showing a variety of penguins. Instruct students to color and cut out the pictures. Then have children tape a two-foot length of yarn to the back of each picture, and make a loop at the top for hanging.

Here are some facts to share with the class about the penguins displayed on their mobiles:

- Emperor penguins are the largest penguins—they stand about four feet tall.
- King penguins may dive as deep as 800 feet—about the height of an 80-story building!
- Macaroni penguins are named for gentlemen who dressed in fancy clothes 200 years ago; these men were called "macaronies."
- Gentoo penguins do not waddle slowly on land; instead, they trot briskly.
- Adelie penguins stand about 18 inches tall; they are one of the smallest penguins.
- Chinstrap penguins get their name from the line that runs below their chins.

Name _____ Date _____

Penguin Maze

Color a path from the father penguin to the mother penguin and chick.

Name _____ Date _____

Penguin Mobile

Color the penguins. Cut them out.
Tape yarn to the back of each penguin.

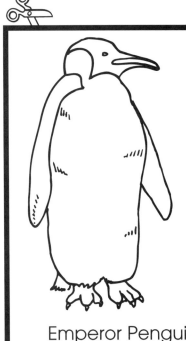
Emperor Penguin

King Penguin

Macaroni Penguin

Gentoo Penguin

Adelie Penguin

Chinstrap Penguin

Penguin Pals

Language Arts and Art Link—Making a visual display

Here's a fun penguin art project for students. Reproduce "Penguin Pal" (page 38) on heavy paper for each child. Each child will need two copies. Have children cut out one of their penguins. Instruct the class to tear bits of black and white tissue paper, scrunch up the pieces, and glue them all over their penguin's bodies. Have students repeat the procedure with orange tissue paper for the beaks and feet. After the penguins are covered, show children how to trim the excess paper.

Next, have each child think of a fact he or she learned about penguins. Let children share their facts with the class, and write them on the board. Have each student copy a penguin fact on his or her second penguin, and then invite them to color the penguins. When the second penguin is completed, display the each child's penguin pals side-by-side on a bulletin board.

Penguin Follow-the-Leader

Physical Education Link—Participating in movement activities

Tell the class that penguins usually travel in groups, often in straight lines that look like they are playing "follow the leader." If possible, show pictures of penguins traveling in this way. (Look in library books or other resources for appropriate pictures.) Have students describe what the penguins look like as they walk, and have them share what they think the animals are doing.

Afterwards, take your class outdoors for a game of "Penguin Follow-the-Leader." Have children take turns being the leader. Encourage leaders to act like penguins, waddling along the pavement with their hands at their sides, hopping down steps, or holding their arms against their faces as if ready to dive.

Name _____ Date _____

Penguin Pal

38 reproducible © Fearon Teacher Aids FE11025

Peppy Penguin Party

Culminating Activity

Wrap up your students' study of penguins with a lively class party. Your class will enjoy helping you prepare the decorations and food. Here are some ideas to get you started:

Decorations
- Hang blue and white paper chains along the wall or chalkboard ledges.
- Cut icicles from aluminum foil, and hang them from the tops of window ledges.
- Make Penguin Pals with tissue paper (see "Penguin Pals" activity on page 37). Tape them to the door, or pin them on a bulletin board.
- Cut paper snowflakes. Tape or hang them around the room.

Food
- Fill paper cups with goldfish crackers.
- Make blue gelatin for an "ocean" dessert. If desired, add white marshmallows for "icebergs."
- Get ready-to-serve drinks that are blue.

Clothing
- Have children dress in black and white clothes. Or, if that is impractical, have students cut out bow ties from black paper, and attach them to children's tops or shirts with safety pins.

Activities
- Play "Fish Concentration." Cut out paper fish. On each one, write a letter or word. Make two fish for each letter and word. Lay the fish facedown on a table or on the floor. Have students take turns picking up two fish at a time. If the letters or words match, the student keeps them. If not, he or she places them back in their original positions. Keep playing until all the fish are matched. The student with the most fish wins.
- Have a "Penguin Egg Relay." Divide the class into teams, and give each team a clay egg. The first person on each team places the egg on his or her feet, waddles to a designated spot, and then runs back with the egg. The second person repeats the procedure, and so on. The first team to have all players waddle and run back wins the game. (Variation: Have students waddle with a rubber ball between their legs.)

© Fearon Teacher Aids FE11025

Unit Four

Backyard Critters

Use this unit to help children explore bugs, butterflies, and more!

Background for Teachers

Here is some information about creatures commonly found around people's homes.

Insects are small, six-legged creatures. Their body is divided into three main parts—head, thorax (middle part), and abdomen. Most insects also have a pair of antennae and wings. There are more than 800,000 insects known so far, but scientists think that that there are millions more yet to be discovered. Insects include ants, bees, butterflies, fleas, and grasshoppers.

Spiders are small creatures that spin silk. Some people mistake spiders for insects, but spiders have eight legs and, unlike insects, they do not have wings or antennae. All spiders spin silk, but they do not all make webs. Spiders are helpful to people because they eat harmful insects.

Earthworms are long, legless animals. Their soft bodies are made up of segments. Earthworms have no lungs or gills; instead, they breathe through their skin. They feed on dead plant materials found in soil. Earthworms are helpful because they help break down humus—the decaying matter in soil. This makes the soil richer and contributes to the growth of plants.

Snails have soft bodies covered by shells. They creep along on a muscular organ called a *foot*. The foot is the part of the snail's body that sticks out of the shell. Snails vary greatly in size. Some are the size of a pinhead, while others grow to be two feet long.

Literature Resources

ABC of Crawlers and Flyers by Hope Ryden (Clarion, 1996). Each letter of the alphabet is represented by a different insect, from an ant to a zebra longwing.

Beekeepers by Linda Oatman High (Boyds Mills, 1998). This book tells how a grandfather and granddaughter move bees into a new hive.

Chirping Crickets by Melvin Berger (HarperCollins, 1998). This book helps children discover how crickets chirp, how they listen with their knees, and more.

Insects Are My Life by Megan McDonald (Orchard, 1997). This story tells about Amanda, a girl who loves bugs.

The Magic Schoolbus Inside a Beehive by Joanna Cole (Scholastic, 1996). Ms. Frizzle's class takes a magical trip inside a beehive.

Monarch Butterfly by Gail Gibbons (Holiday, 1991). This delightful book explores the life cycle of the Monarch butterfly.

Looking at Insects

Science Link—Identifying the characteristics of insects

Ask students to name some of the small creatures they see in their yards. Write their responses on the board. Then circle all the insect names that were listed. Tell the class that these animals are called *insects.*

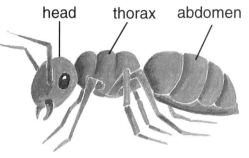

Draw three ovals to make a rough sketch of an insect, as shown. Explain that an insect is a small animal with three body parts: head, thorax (middle part), and abdomen (back part). Next, add antennae on the head, and point out that many insects have two feelers on their head called *antennae*. Tell students that insects use their antennae mainly to smell and feel. Add three pairs of legs to the thorax, and tell the class that insects have six legs. Explain that when insects walk, they move the middle leg of one side and the front and back legs of the other side at the same time; in this way, they are balanced and supported, much like a three-legged stool.

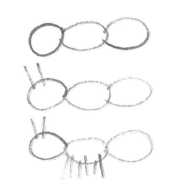

For a follow-up activity, show various pictures of small creatures, such as spiders, beetles, worms, and bees. Ask students to point out which ones are insects and tell how they know. Then give students copies of "Parts of an Insect" (page 42) and "Insect Hunt" (page 43) to complete on their own. (All the animals on page 43 will be colored except for the spider, earthworm, and snail.)

Backyard Bug Hunt

Science Link—Observing insects and other small outdoor creatures

Have students do this activity for homework. Give each child a magnifying glass and a sheet of paper. Tell them to search outside their homes for bugs and other small creatures. Remind students to look between blades of grass and underneath rocks for hidden bugs. Have children examine the creatures with their magnifying glasses and write a list or draw pictures on their papers to record what they find. Afterwards, have children bring their papers to school.

Invite children to share their findings and discuss the following questions:

- Which animals on your list are insects? How do you know?
- Which animal did you see most?
- What do you think the animals were doing?
- Which animal seemed the most interesting?

Name _____ Date _____

Parts of an Insect

Cut out the labels. Glue them in the correct places.

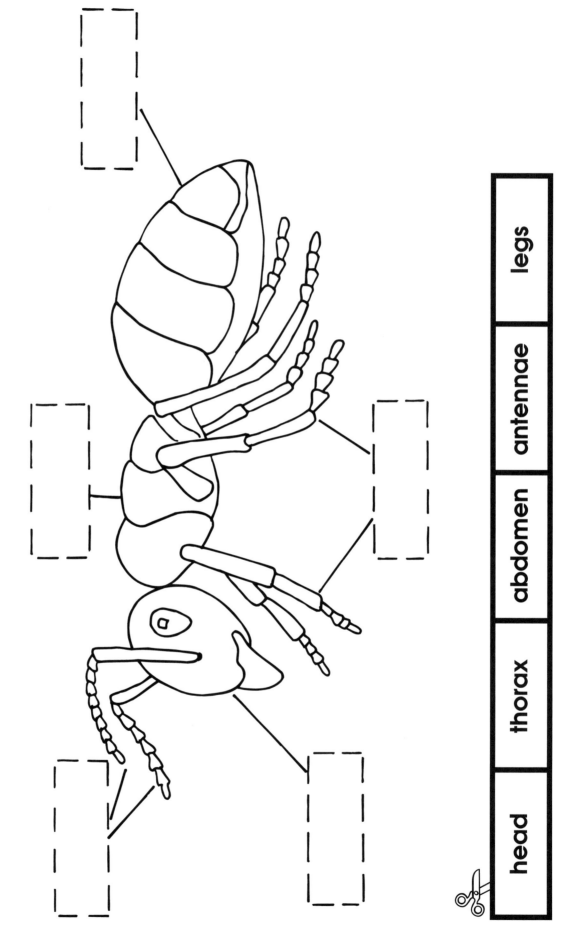

| head | thorax | abdomen | antennae | legs |

Insect Hunt

An insect has three body parts and six legs. Color the insects below.

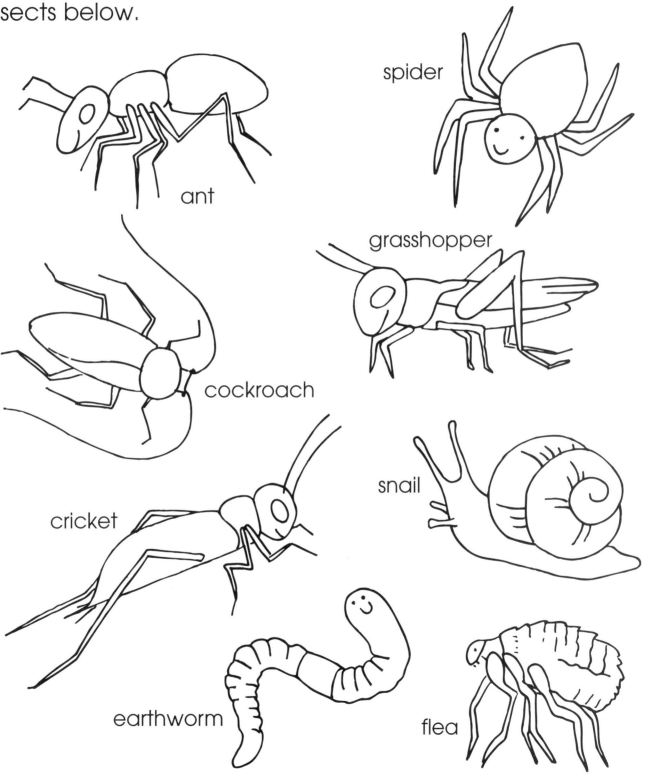

Staying Safe

Science Link—Recognizing how insects protect themselves

Tell the class that insects have many enemies. Explain that birds and other animals hunt insects for food. Ask students how creatures as small as insects can protect themselves from larger hunters. Let students brainstorm ideas, and write their responses on the board.

Show the class pictures of insects protecting themselves in various ways. Discuss the features of each one. Here are some examples:

- Ants have powerful jaws that can pinch.
- Bees and wasps have poisonous stings.
- Many butterflies and moths have wings with colors that blend in with their surroundings.
- Inchworms and some caterpillars look like twigs.
- Some butterflies have bright colors or scary-looking markings that warn animals to stay away. For example, the owl butterfly has markings that look like large eyes.

For a follow-up activity, give students a copy of "My Mini-Book About Insects Staying Safe" (page 45). Have students color and cut out the pages. Then have them staple the pages together in order to make a mini-book about insects staying safe.

Life Cycle of a Butterfly

Science Link—Recognizing that the butterfly goes through a great change while growing up

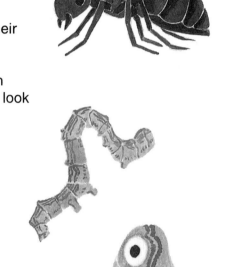

Talk with your students about how they looked when they were born, how they look now, and how they think they will look as adults. Discuss the various changes that take place as a person grows (Examples: *gets taller, gains weight, face shape changes*). Tell students that the butterfly goes through amazing changes as it grows up. Then discuss the four stages in the life cycle of a butterfly:

- The butterfly starts life as an egg.
- The butterfly hatches as a larva (caterpillar). It eats and grows quickly.
- After about two weeks, the caterpillar reaches its full size and changes into a pupa. The pupa is covered with a hard shell. The shell hangs from a twig.
- The adult butterfly comes out of the shell.

If possible, share with the class some library books that show how the butterfly develops. Then reproduce "Life Cycle of a Butterfly" (page 46) for each child, and have children cut and glue the pictures to review the four stages in a butterfly's life.

My Mini-Book About Insects Staying Safe

Name _____

1

A bee stings its enemies.

2

An ant pinches with its jaws.

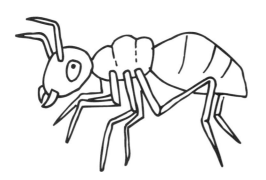

3

An inchworm looks like a twig and hides.

4

A butterfly may have scary markings.

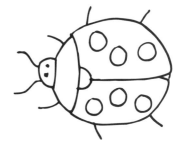

5

A ladybug's bright red color warns animals to stay away.

Name_____   Date_____

Life Cycle of a Butterfly

There are four stages in a butterfly's life. Look at the pictures at the bottom of the page. Cut them out. Glue them to the correct places on the circle.

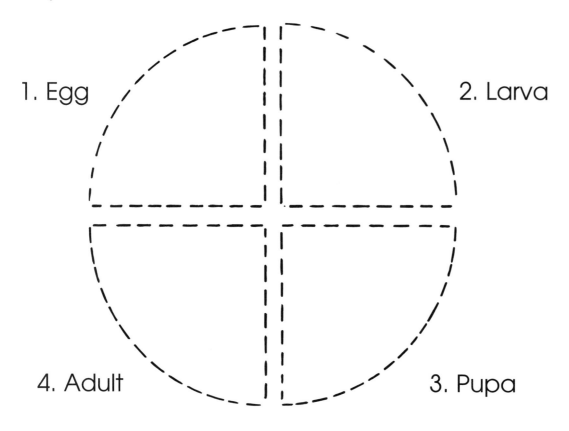

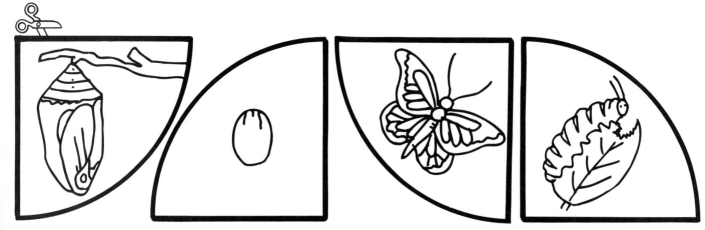

46 reproducible © Fearon Teacher Aids FE11025

Butterfly Wings

Math Link—Understanding that one half of a butterfly looks like the mirror image of the other half

Show pictures of butterflies with interesting wings. Have students notice the colors and patterns on the wings. Point out that the wings on one side of a butterfly looks like the wings on the other side. Then do this simple demonstration. You will need a small, rectangular mirror. You will also need to draw half a butterfly on a small sheet of paper. (See diagram.)

Hold the mirror perpendicular to the butterfly's body, and show how a mirror image of the drawing appears. Let students take turns holding the mirror to the drawing; they will see a mirror image of the picture, and the butterfly will look "whole." Tell students that if they folded a butterfly's wings together, the colors and patterns would match. (If you wish, introduce the term *symmetrical* to the class.) Afterwards, give students a copy of "Butterfly Wings" (page 48), and let them decorate the wings to make their own symmetrical butterflies.

Funny Critters

Math Link—Measuring length

Review measurement with this activity. Give each child a copy of "Funny Critters" (page 49), and ask the class to cut out the rulers at the bottoms of the pages. Tell students that the ruler is six inches long, and that each of its sections is one inch long. If needed, demonstrate how to use the ruler and its markings to find out the length of an object. Then have students use the ruler to measure the critters, and tell them to record their answers on the lines.

Afterwards, discuss results with the class. Ask the following questions: *Which critter is the longest? Which is the shortest? Which critter is about the same length as your middle finger?*

Answers: A) two inches, B) three inches, C) one inch, D) four inches, E) five inches

© Fearon Teacher Aids FE11025

Name _____ Date _____

Butterfly Wings

Color the wings so that one half of the butterfly matches the other half.

48 reproducible © Fearon Teacher Aids FE11025

Name _____ Date _____

Funny Critters

Cut out the ruler at the bottom of the page. Use it to measure how long each critter is. Write your answers on the lines.

A.  ____ inches

B.  ____ inches

C.  ____ inch

D.  ____ inches

E. 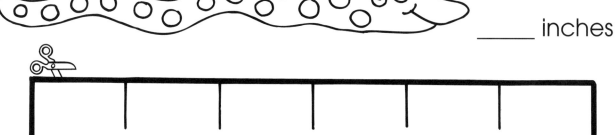 ____ inches

Snail Trails

Science and Math Link—Making observations, and measuring duration of time

Purchase some live snails from a pet store, and place them in an aquarium. Let students watch the snails, and see if they can observe the following facts:

- A snail has a soft body.
- A snail has a coiled shell.
- A snail moves very slowly.
- A snail creeps along on the bottom part of its body (on a muscular organ called the *foot*).
- A snail may have a spiral-shaped shell.
- Some snail shells come in beautiful colors.

Your students will enjoy watching a "snail race." Choose two snails from your aquarium. Place the snails on a sheet of black paper, and let them go! Have children time the snails to see how long it takes for them to move to one end of the paper. As the animals crawl, have students observe shiny tracks, or trails. Explain that this sticky slime helps snails move.

Earthworm Shapes

Math Link—Identifying and making geometric shapes

Show the class pictures of earthworms. Tell students that earthworms have smooth bodies made up of rings. Add that earthworms do not have eyes or ears; instead, they have mouths that are sensitive to heat, light, and touch. Tell the class that earthworms eat dead plant material found in soil.

Have students describe what earthworms look like when they move (they wriggle, they curl). Tell children that they will be making their own earthworms to play with. Then give each child a small ball of clay. Have children make earthworms by rubbing the clay between their palms to make wormlike shapes at least six inches long. Say the following: *Our earthworms are very smart. They have been to school and they know their shapes, just like you do!* Then have students make their earthworms into the following shapes: *circle, square, triangle, rectangle.*

(Variation: Hold up several objects, and have students make their earthworms into numbers that show how many objects are on display.)

Spider Treat

Language Arts Link—Following oral directions

Display several pictures of spiders, and ask children why spiders are not insects. Guide them to seeing that spiders have eight legs instead of six. Then let the class make some yummy treats to help them remember that fact.

First, give each child a small paper plate, a plastic spoon, a cracker, a tablespoon of peanut butter, some raisins, and eight pretzel sticks. Then have children listen carefully and follow your oral directions:

1. Put the cracker in the middle of your plate.
2. Use the plastic spoon to spread peanut butter on the cracker.
3. Add two raisins for eyes.
4. Add pretzel sticks around the cracker for legs. Count to make sure you have the right amount of legs.
5. Eat your spider treat!

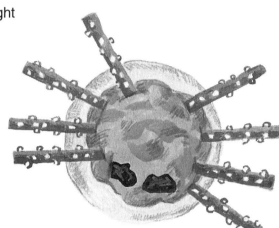

Musical Bees

Music Link—Playing a simple game

Tell students that bees fly around in search of food. Explain that they look for nectar, a sugary liquid made inside flowers. Tell the class that bees are especially attracted to the colors *yellow* and *purple,* so flowers with these colors attract bees easily.

Next, tell children to imagine they are bees in search of colorful flowers, and have them play this fun version of "Musical Chairs." Arrange the chairs around your classroom so you have one chair for every child. Place purple paper squares and yellow paper squares on all the chairs except two. Tell students that the chairs with the paper squares represent flowers.

Then play a musical recording, and have children "buzz" around the room. When the music stops, children sit in the chairs. The two children whose chairs do not have a purple or yellow square are out of the game. For the next round, remove two chairs that have paper squares, and repeat the procedure. Keep playing until you only have two children left in the game. For the final round, leave one chair with a paper square and one chair without. Play and then stop the music. The child who sits on the chair with the paper square wins the game.

© Fearon Teacher Aids FE11025

Unit Five

Tide Pool World

Add a splash of fun to your classroom with tide pool tales and activities!

Background for Teachers

Tide pools form where pools of water collect in rocky hollows at low tide. They are a refuge for plants and animals that cannot live in the open air when the tide goes out. Animals living in tide pools must be hardy. In order to survive, they must keep from being washed away by the waves at high tide; keep from drying out in the sun at low tide; and keep from being eaten. A variety of animals live in tide pools, including:

Crabs come in many varieties. Some are oval-shaped, while others are rectangular or triangular. Crabs have two strong claws. They climb up on their back legs and hold out their claws to protect themselves. If a crab loses a claw, it grows a new one. Many crabs live under or between rocks.

Mussels have soft bodies and hard shells. Their shells are made up of two pieces called *valves*. These valves are joined by a hinge, and they open and close. Mussels anchor themselves to rocks so the waves do not wash them out of the tide pool.

Sea anemones look like flowers. They have cylinder-shaped bodies with many tentacles on top. These tentacles surround the mouth. Sea anemones catch small animals by poisoning them with their tentacles, and then using the tentacles to drag the prey into their mouths.

Sea stars, also called **starfish**, usually have five arms. Each arm has rows of tiny tube feet. Sea stars grip rocks with the suckers on their tube feet. The arms are strong enough to pull open clam shells. If a sea star is cut in half, it can grow into two sea stars.

Literature Resources

Exploring an Ocean Tide Pool by Jeanne Bendick (Holt, 1995). This book introduces young readers to how its plant and animal inhabitants live and function together.

Harmonica Night by M. C. Helldorfer (Atheneum, 1997). In this story, a little boy and his grandmother spend late night hours on the beach and share a magical midnight adventure.

Life in a Tide Pool by Allan Fowler (Children's Press, 1996). Children discover how tide pools form, and learn about the plants and animals that live there.

Sea Stars and Dragons by Phyllis Jean Perry (Watt, 1996). The author describes the characteristics of starfish and seahorses.

Where the Waves Break: Life at the Edge of the Sea by Anita Malnig (Carolrhoda Books, 1987). This photo-illustrated book examines the various marine animals and plants found along the edge of the sea.

Tide Pool Model

Science Link—Making a model of a tide pool

Ask students if they have ever been to the seashore. Ask if they have ever observed the waves. Elicit from students the fact that the waves come in and go out on a regular basis. Tell students that when the waves come way up on the shoreline, it is called *high tide.* When the waves only reach a short distance up the shoreline, it is called *low tide.*

Explain that when the tide goes out, sometimes small pools of water are left behind. Tell students that these pools are called *tide pools.* Explain that a tide pool contains a community of plants and animals that would not survive in the open air. Some of the animals in a tide pool swim freely in the water; some are attached to rocks; some live only at the bottom of the tide pool.

Next, let students help you make a model of a tide pool. Cover the bottom of a large tub with sand. Fill the tub until it is half full. Then have students contribute items for the tide pool. Here are some ideas:

- rocks
- shells
- plastic toys of crabs, sea stars, and other small sea creatures
- plastic seaweed

Afterwards, give students a copy of "Tide Pool" (page 54) to complete.

Waves in Action

Science Link—Observing how the action of waves affects a tide pool

Do the following experiment with children to demonstrate why most creatures that live in tide pools must have special features that enable them to cling tightly to the shore.

First, prop one end of a baking pan on a book or other object so it is raised about one or two inches. Then place a few rocks in the pan. Tell students that the pan represents a tide pool. Then pour water into the pan until it reaches about halfway up the pan. Move a piece of cardboard back and forth in the pan to create "waves." Have students observe what happens. (The rocks move around.) Ask what might happen to the animals in a tide pool whenever waves come in. (The animals would be washed away or hurt on the rocks by the waves.) Tell students that animals that live in tide pools have special features to help them cling to the shore.

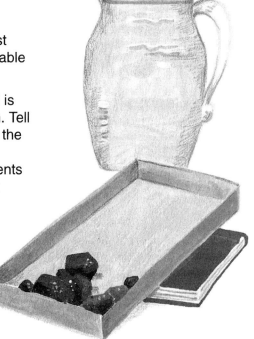

Tide Pool

Find these animals in the tide pool and color them.

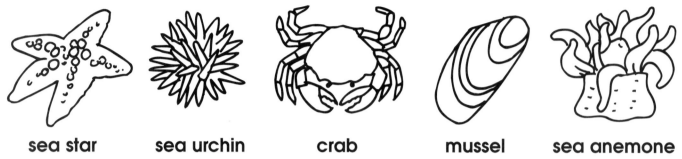

sea star   sea urchin   crab   mussel   sea anemone

Hanging On

Science Link—Recognizing ways that tide pool creatures adapt to their environment

Do this activity after your class has done the "Waves in Action" activity on page 53. Review with students that the movement of waves causes jarring in the tide pool. Animals would be thrown against the rocks or washed away if they did not have any ways to protect themselves. Tell students that tide pool animals have special features that help them cling to the shore when the waves move in and out. Then show them pictures of the animals mentioned below (use library books and other resources), and discuss the following information:

- A **snail**'s foot (the muscular organ on which it moves) holds it fast to one spot.
- A **mussel** attaches itself to a rock with strong, leathery threads.
- **Sea stars**, **sea urchins**, and **sea anemones** have suction cups that allow them to cling to rocks.
- A **barnacle** uses "cement" that it makes with its body to attach itself to a rock.

If possible, bring samples of the animals for the class to see. (For example, you may be able to get some mussels from a place that sells seafood.) Then give students a copy of "My Mini-Book About Creatures 'Hanging On'" (page 56). Have children color the pictures, cut out the pages, and staple them together in order to make a mini-book about the special features of tide pool creatures.

Crab Skeleton

Science Link—Recognizing how a crab's body protects it in its tide pool environment

Show the children a picture of a crab. If possible, bring in a crab or some crab legs from a seafood shop. Tell students that unlike a mussel or sea star (see "Hanging On" activity above), a crab does not cling to the shore when the waves come in and go out. Instead, it is protected by its shell if it is thrown against the rocks. If you have your crab sample, pass it around for children to touch. Ask questions such as: *How does the shell feel? What do you think is the purpose of the shell?*

Next, ask students where their skeleton is (inside their body). Ask what their skeleton is made up of (bones). Tell the class that a skeleton helps protects the body's organs (such as the heart, brain, and lungs). Explain that a crab has no such bones; instead, its soft inner parts are protected by the shell. Tell students that the shell is really the animal's skeleton. Add that the shell is called the *exoskeleton,* a word meaning that the skeleton is on the outside of the body. Then have students complete page 57, "Crab Skeleton" for a follow-up activity.

© Fearon Teacher Aids FE11025

My Mini-Book About
Creatures "Hanging On"

Name _____

1

Tide pool animals have special ways to hang on to the shore when the waves come and go.

2

These animals have suckers that let them cling to rocks.

3

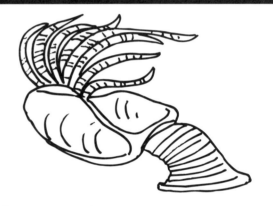

A barnacle uses a "cement" to attach itself to a rock.

4

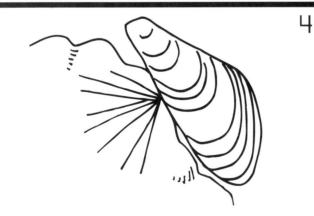

A mussel clings to rocks with strong, leathery threads.

5

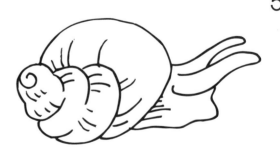

A snail's "foot" (on the bottom of its body) holds it in one place.

Name _____ Date _____

Crab Skeleton

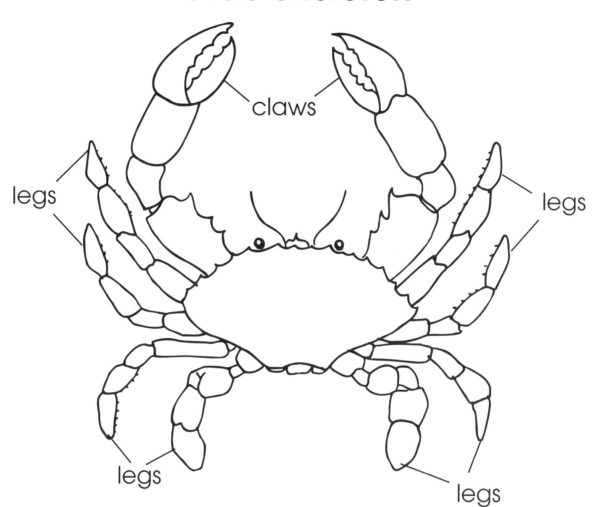

Circle the answers.

1. Where is the crab's skeleton?   inside   outside
2. Where is your skeleton?   inside   outside
3. Is a crab's skeleton hard or soft?   hard   soft
4. Is your skeleton hard or soft?   hard   soft
5. How many claws does a crab have?   two   four
6. Who has more legs—person or crab?   person   crab

Who's Hiding in the Tide Pool?

Math Link—Solving addition problems

Use the activity sheet on page 59 to review basic addition facts. Instruct students to complete the problems first, and then have them color the spaces in the puzzle according to the directions. When the spaces are filled in, children will find a hidden tide pool creature.

Tide Pool Take-Away

Math Link—Solving story problems involving subtraction

Let your class practice subtraction problems with these tide pool tales. Have students solve the problems with beans, pieces of paper, or other counters.

A. There were 6 crabs playing in the sand. Then 3 crabs went to hide under a rock. How many crabs were left in the sand?

B. There were 10 sea snails crawling along the bottom of the tide pool. A child came and scooped up 3 snails to look at them. How many snails were left at the bottom of the tide pool?

C. A boy found 9 shells. He gave 4 shells to a friend. How many shells did he have left?

D. A girl lifted a rock and found 6 crabs. A boy lifted a rock and found 2 crabs. How many more crabs did the girl find than the boy?

E. There were 7 sea urchins on one rock. There were 3 sea urchins on another rock. How many more sea urchins were on the first rock than on the second one?

Continue making up other story problems about tide pool creatures. Or, have students make up problems, too; let them challenge the class to solve the problems.

Name _____ Date _____

Who's Hiding in the Tide Pool?

Write the answers to the problems. Use the answers to color the spaces.

1, 2, 3—Color blue
4, 5, 6—Color brown
7, 8, 9—Color orange

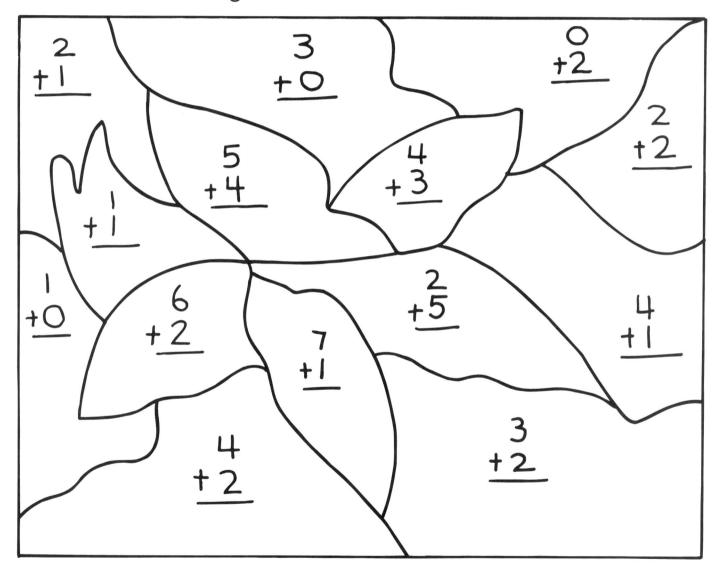

Who is hiding? Circle your answer.

crab   sea star   snail

Tide Pool Sing-Along

Music Link—Singing a song and acting out the words

Teach your students the following song about two tide pool creatures:

> **I Am Living in a Tide Pool**
> (Sing to the tune of "I've Been Working on the Railroad".)
>
> I am living in a tide pool, where the tide rolls in,
> I'm a crusty little sea star, with a crusty little grin!
> Holding, holding on so tightly
> To the rocks at noon,
> Hoping, hoping that some dinner floats by
> very soon.
>
> I am living in a tide pool, where the tide rolls out,
> I'm a pretty little sea snail, I like to crawl about,
> Creeping, creeping, oh so slowly,
> But at a steady pace.
> And when the water pounds my foothold
> It helps me keep in place.

Have students color the sea star and sea snail pictures on page 61, "Tide Pool Sing-Along." Instruct them to cut out the pictures and glue them to craft sticks. Then have children sing the song again, but this time let them hold up the appropriate animal when singing each verse.

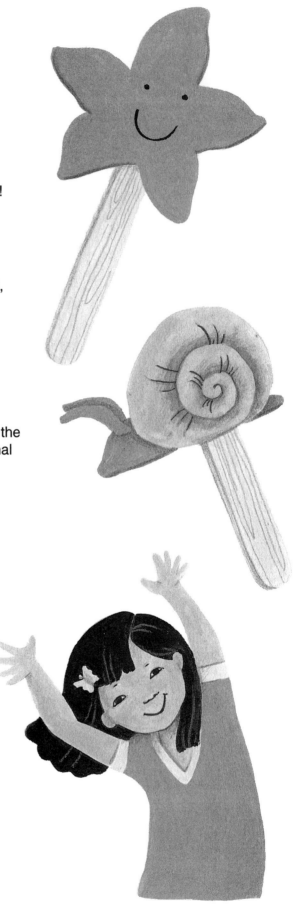

Tide In and Tide Out

Movement Link—Singing a song and acting out the words

Tell the class that when the tide comes in and fills the tide pool, some animals are busy catching food and eating; when the tide goes out, the animals rest. Then play this fun game with children. When you call out *Tide in,* children pretend to collect food. Tell them to pretend they are specific animals. For example, sea anemones reach up with their tentacles and catch small animals that swim by; crabs scurry around; and sea stars use their tube feet (slender tubes on the undersides of their bodies) to crack open shelled animals such as clams and mussels. When you call out *Tide out,* children stop moving and stay still.

Name _____ Date _____

Tide Pool Sing-Along

Color the pictures. Cut them out. Glue each picture to a craft stick.

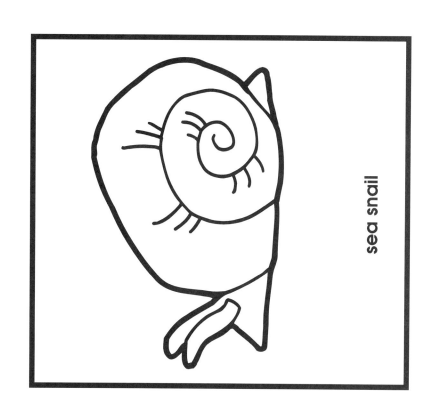

sea snail

sea star

© Fearon Teacher Aids FE11025

Tide Pool Open House

Culminating Activity

Have students make a colorful tide pool display in your classroom, and then invite other students to visit for a Tide Pool Open House. Begin by covering a table with a large sheet of blue paper. Tape plastic wrap on top to make the table shimmer like water. Ask each child to bring a rock from home to place around the water's edge to form the tide pool. You may wish to spread a thin layer of sand in some areas of the tide pool as well.

Next, divide your class into "tide pool teams." Assign each team one of the following projects (each child can make one or more of the assigned crafts):

Stuffed Sea Stars
Give students patterns to cut out large sea stars from heavy paper. Have children color two sea stars and staple them along the edges, leaving an opening. Instruct them to stuff the sea stars with small, crumpled pieces of newspaper. Staple the sea stars shut.

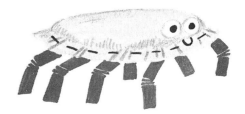

Paper Plate Crabs
Have students color or paint two six-inch paper plates. Staple the plates together to make the crab's body. Have students tape on legs and claws made from pipe cleaners or straws (bendable straws work well for jointed legs).

Egg Carton Sea Snails
Have students form a snail's body from clay. Then give each child an egg carton cup for the snail's shell. Have students paint the cups, and then have them glue the cups on the backs of the bodies.

Salt Dough Sea Urchins
Make a salt dough mixture, and have students make a rounded body. Then while the dough is still soft, have students stick toothpicks all over the body. Let the dough dry for several days. Afterwards, spray-paint the sea urchins.

Salt Dough: Mix 2½ cups flour with ⅝ cup salt. Add about ¾ cup water, a little at a time, and mix well. Add more water if the dough is too stiff. On a floured board, knead the dough for one minute. Store the flour in a plastic bag, and keep refrigerated.

Tide Pool Plants
Have students cut out seaweed and other plants from paper or stiff fabric. Students can also cut lengths of yarn and spray them with starch to stiffen them.

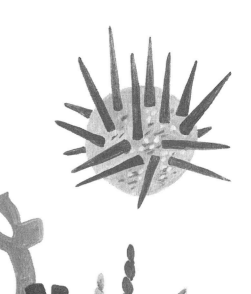

Notes